Barclay

by Iain Gray

PUBLISHING

WRITING *to* REMEMBER

WRITING *to* REMEMBER

79 Main Street, Newtongrange,
Midlothian EH22 4NA
Tel: 0131 344 0414
E-mail: info@lang-syne.co.uk
www.langsyneshop.co.uk

Design by Dorothy Meikle
Printed by Printwell Ltd
© Lang Syne Publishers Ltd 2023

All rights reserved. No part of this publication may be reproduced, stored or introduced into a retrieval system, or transmitted in any form or by any means (electronic, mechanical, photocopying, recording or otherwise) without the prior written permission of Lang Syne Publishers Ltd.

ISBN 978-1-85217-784-3

Barclay

MOTTO:
Either action or death

CREST:
Out of a chapeau,
a hand grasping a dagger

TERRITORY:
Aberdeenshire and Kincardineshire

NAME variations include:
Berclay
Berkeley
Berkley

Chapter one:

The origins of popular surnames

by George Forbes and Iain Gray

If you don't know where you came from, you won't know where you're going **is a frequently quoted observation and one that has a particular resonance today when there has been a marked upsurge in interest in genealogy, with increasing numbers of people curious to trace their family roots.**

Main sources for genealogical research include census returns and official records of births, marriages and deaths – and the key to unlocking the detail they contain is obviously a family surname, one that has been 'inherited' and passed from generation to generation.

No matter our station in life, we all have a surname – but it was not until about the middle of the fourteenth century that the practice of being identified by a particular surname became commonly established throughout the British Isles.

Previous to this, it was normal for a person to be identified through the use of only a forename.

But as population gradually increased and there were many more people with the same forename, surnames were adopted to distinguish one person, or community, from another.

Many common English surnames are patronymic in origin, meaning they stem from the forename of one's father – with 'Johnson,' for example, indicating 'son of John.'

It was the Normans, in the wake of their eleventh century conquest of Anglo-Saxon England, a pivotal moment in the nation's history, who first brought surnames into usage – although it was a gradual process.

For the Normans, these were names initially based on the title of their estates, local villages and chateaux in France to distinguish and identify these landholdings.

Such grand descriptions also helped enhance the prestige of these warlords and generally glorify their lofty positions high above the humble serfs slaving away below in the pecking order who had only single names, often with Biblical connotations as in Pierre and Jacques.

The only descriptive distinctions among the peasantry concerned their occupations, like 'Pierre the swineherd' or 'Jacques the ferryman.'

Roots of surnames that came into usage in England not only included Norman-French, but also Old French, Old Norse, Old English, Middle English, German, Latin, Greek, Hebrew and the Gaelic languages of the Celts.

The Normans themselves were originally Vikings, or 'Northmen', who raided, colonised and eventually settled down around the French coastline.

They had sailed up the Seine in their longboats in 900AD under their ferocious leader Rollo and ruled the roost in north eastern France before sailing over to conquer England in 1066 under Duke William of Normandy – better known to posterity as William the Conqueror, or King William I of England.

Granted lands in the newly-conquered England, some of their descendants later acquired territories in Wales, Scotland and Ireland – taking not only their own surnames, but also the practice of adopting a surname, with them.

But it was in England where Norman rule and custom first impacted, particularly in relation to the adoption of surnames.

This is reflected in the famous *Domesday Book*, a massive survey of much of England and Wales, ordered by William I, to determine who owned what, what it was worth and therefore how much they were liable to pay in taxes to the voracious Royal Exchequer.

Completed in 1086 and now held in the National Archives in Kew, London, 'Domesday' was an Old English word meaning 'Day of Judgement.'

This was because, in the words of one contemporary chronicler, "its decisions, like those of the Last Judgement, are unalterable."

It had been a requirement of all those English landholders – from the richest to the poorest – that they identify themselves for the purposes of the survey and for future reference by means of a surname.

This is why the *Domesday Book*, although written in Latin as was the practice for several centuries with both civic and ecclesiastical records, is an invaluable source for the early appearance of a wide range of English surnames.

Several of these names were coined in connection with occupations.

These include Baker and Smith, while Cooks, Chamberlains, Constables and Porters were to be found carrying out duties in large medieval households.

The church's influence can be found in names such as Bishop, Friar and Monk while the popular name of Bennett derives from the late fifth to mid-sixth century Saint Benedict, founder of the Benedictine order of monks.

The early medical profession is represented by Barber, while businessmen produced names that include Merchant and Sellers.

Down at the village watermill, the names that cropped up included Millar/Miller, Walker and Fuller, while other self-explanatory trades included Cooper, Tailor, Mason and Wright.

Even the scenery was utilised as in Moor, Hill, Wood and Forrest – while the hunt and the chase supplied names that include Hunter, Falconer, Fowler and Fox.

Colours are also a source of popular surnames, as in Black, Brown, Gray/Grey, Green and White, and would have denoted the colour of the clothing the person habitually wore or, apart from the obvious exception of 'Green', one's hair colouring or even complexion.

The surname Red developed into Reid, while

Blue was rare and no-one wanted to be associated with yellow.

Rather self-important individuals took surnames that include Goodman and Wiseman, while physical attributes crept into surnames such as Small and Little.

Many families proudly boast the heraldic device known as a Coat of Arms, as featured on our front cover.

The central motif of the Coat of Arms would originally have been what was sometimes borne on the shield of a warrior to distinguish himself from others on the battlefield.

Not featured on the Coat of Arms, but highlighted on page three, are the family motto and related crest – with the latter frequently different from the central motif.

Adding further variety to the rich cultural heritage that is represented by surnames is the appearance in recent times in lists of the most common names found throughout the United Kingdom of ones that include Khan, Patel and Singh – names that have proud roots in the vast sub-continent of India.

Echoes of a far distant past can still be found in our surnames and they can be borne with pride in commemoration of our forebears.

Chapter two:

On the field of battle

A surname whose presence in Scotland has long been the subject of debate, 'Barclay', a form of 'Berkeley' or 'Berkly', features prominently in the frequently turbulent historical record.

What is not in dispute is that those who came to bear the name were of original Norman stock, settling first in England in the wake of the Conquest of 1066 under William of Normandy.

Following his defeat of King Harold II, the last Anglo-Saxon king, William was declared monarch and the complete subjugation of his subjects followed, with those Normans who had fought on his behalf rewarded with their lands.

One tradition is that the Scottish Barclays descend from the Anglo-Norman Earls of Berkeley who, in 1153, built Berkeley Castle, in Gloucestershire – and that some members of this family settled later in the century in Aberdeenshire and Fife.

Another theory is that the 'Berkeleys/Berkleys' – later 'Barclays' – took their name from the village of Berkely, in Somerset, and that it was members of this family, including a Walter and Robert de (of) Berkely who subsequently settled in Scotland.

The consensus of opinion now is that there were two separate 'migrations' to Scotland of those who would come to take the Barclay name.

This explains why over the centuries there arose two distinct families of the name, with only a loose bond of kinship – the Barclays of Towie, in the Aberdeenshire parish of Turriff and the Barclays of Mathers, Kincardineshire.

Of the line which became the Barclays of Mathers – later the Barclays of Mathers and Urie – and in the form of 'Berkley', Sir Walter Berkley, a grandson of his namesake Walter Berkeley, 3rd Laird of Gartly, in Strathbogie, Aberdeenshire, served from 1165 to 1189 in the powerful post of Chancellor of Scotland.

The eighth laird, also named Walter, appears as a signatory to an infamous document of 1296.

In July of that year, the Scots had risen in revolt against the imperialist designs of England's King Edward I.

But, following his crushing of the rising led by the freedom fighter William Wallace, he brought the entire nation under his subjugation little less than a month later, garrisoning strategic locations and demanding the signing of a humiliating treaty of fealty.

Reluctantly ascribed to at Berwick by 1,500 Scottish earls, bishops and burgesses, the parchment is known as the *Ragman Roll* because of the profusion of ribbons that dangle from the seals of the signatories – among whom was Walter Berkely, 8th Laird of Gartly.

In common with many others who had been forced to sign the roll, he later redeemed himself by taking up arms in defence of Scotland's freedom and independence under the great warrior king Robert the Bruce.

Another reluctant signatory to the *Ragman Roll* was Sir David Barclay, Sheriff of Fife, who also rallied to Bruce – dying for the nation's cause at the battle of Bannockburn in June of 1314.

While early bearers of the name and its various spelling variants gained distinction on the battlefield, one particularly unsavoury character was George Berclay, 5th Laird of Mathers.

A thorn in the flesh to Berclay and other lairds who frequently flouted the law, was John Melville of Glenbervie, Sheriff of the Mearns, Kincardineshire.

In addition to acting with zeal in performance

of his legal duties, he was also considered arrogant – and these traits combined to make him hated.

So loathed was he that, in 1421, Berclay and two of his uncles and other lairds embarked on a truly murderous course of action to rid themselves of him.

For many years, Murdoch, Duke of Albany, the sheriff's immediate superior, had endured frequent complaints about his behaviour and unwittingly gave the green light for his murder by exclaiming in exasperation: *"Sorrow gin (if) that sheriff were sodden (drowned) and supped in broo (broth)"*.

Taking this as a cue for action, Berclay and his accomplices invited the unsuspecting Melville to a great feast in a forest where a large fire and bubbling cauldron of water had already been prepared.

Seized and stripped, he was thrown into the cauldron and, after being boiled for a lengthy time, the gleeful murderers all enjoyed a spoonful of the resultant 'soup'.

Despite the horrific nature of the crime, these were particularly cruel and vicious times and Berclay was later pardoned for the deed.

Firmly established by the seventeenth century in the shipping trade between Scotland, Scandinavia and the lands around the Baltic, the Barclays of Towie took their name from the small hamlet of Towie – also known as 'Tolly', or 'Towy' – on the River Don, Aberdeenshire.

Their most famous son is one whose memory is honoured to this day as having been instrumental in the defeat of French Emperor Napoleon Bonaparte, whose army invaded Russia in 1812.

Known as Field Marshall Barclay de Tolly or Prince Michael Andreas de Tolly, he was born in 1761 in Lithuania, then part of the Russian Empire, and where his family of the Barclays of Towie originally settled as merchants.

With his father the first to be accepted into the privileged and glittering ranks of the Russian nobility, de Tolly was aged only fifteen when, set on a military career, he joined the Imperial Russian Army, enlisting in a carabineer regiment.

His military skills and acumen, that would later see him rise to the rank of general and then field marshall, came quickly to the fore and in 1788 he was personally decorated by Grigory Potemkin, statesman and favourite of Catherine the Great, for his role in the capture of Ochakov from the Ottomans.

Appointed Governor-General of the Grand Duchy of Finland in recognition of his actions during the Finnish War of 1808 to 1809, by 1810 he had become Minister of War for the Russian Empire.

When Napoleon invaded, in addition to de Tolly's role of Minister of War, he also took on the added responsibility of the 1st Army of the West, the largest Russian army to face the French.

Further promoted to Commander-in-Chief, Barclay de Tolly was in command of both the centre and right wing of the army at the battle of Borodino in September of 1812 – which resulted in no clear victory for either side.

Harrying the French during their disastrous retreat from Moscow over the frozen steppes and also leading his army in the taking of Paris in 1814, Barclay de Tolly became a national hero.

Promoted to field marshall and elevated to the Order of St George and the Order of St Andrew, this famous descendant of the Barclays of Towie died in 1818, while he is honoured to this day through a number of memorials that include a statue in front of Kazan Cathedral, St Petersburg.

Towie Barclay Castle, meanwhile, built by the Barclays in 1593 on lands they had held from the eleventh century and about 4.5 miles (7.24km) from Turriff, was once feared as holding a curse that affected the clan's male line.

This is apparently the reason it was sold in 1753 to the Earl of Findlater who, in turn, believing the curse to be true after his son died, sold it in 1792 to Robert Gordon's Hospital, Aberdeen.

Having fallen into a state of disrepair by the mid-twentieth century, it was bought and restored in the 1970s by the English folk musician Marc Ellington, born in 1945 in Boston, Lincolnshire and who has performed with bands including Fairport Convention and Matthew's Southern Comfort.

With his wife Karen, a landscaper and garden designer acting as project manager, the castle was restored to such high standard it received a Saltire Award in recognition.

Meanwhile Peter Charles Barclay of Towie Barclay and that Ilk is recognised as 'Chief of the Name and Arms of Barclay and Representer of the House of Towie Barclay'.

Chapter three:

Quakers and entrepreneurs

One famous dynasty of the Barclay name descends from Colonel David Barclay, son of David Barclay, 11th Laird of Mathers.

Born at Mathers in 1610, in common with many other adventurous Scots of his time he plied his trade as a mercenary in foreign lands.

Arriving in Germany when aged only 16, his talents on the field of battle were such that he rose to the rank of major in the army of Gustavus Adolphus, King of Sweden, during the Thirty Years War of 1618 to 1648.

When he returned to Scotland in 1636, the country was in turmoil because of the bitter and bloody wars between Crown and Covenant and, fighting as a Covenanter, served with distinction in a regiment commanded by fellow Scot General John Middleton who was later created 1st Earl of Middleton by King Charles II.

In 1647 he added to the already extensive

family landholdings in Kincardineshire by purchasing the lands and barony of Urie from William Keith, 7th Earl Marischal of Scotland.

But owing to the complex political machinations of the time, with constantly shifting loyalties and allegiances, the earl later fell foul of the authorities and was imprisoned for a time.

A victim of guilt through association, Colonel Barclay was also imprisoned – and it was while being held in confinement in Edinburgh Castle that he underwent a religious conversion.

This, it transpired, was to have important consequences for his descendants in the way in which they conducted not only their private lives but also their business affairs.

The faith he embraced was that of the Quakers, also known as the Christian denomination the Religious Society of Friends.

Founded only a few years before Barclay's conversion by the Leicestershire weaver's son Charles Fox, its adherents were distinguished by their plain dress, teetotalism, refusal to swear oaths and participate in wars and opposition to slavery.

He died in 1686, while he was the father – through his first marriage to Katherine Gordon, daughter of Sir Robert Gordon, 1st Baronet and founder of the Gordonstoun Estate in Moray and his second to Louisa Gordon of London – of three sons and two daughters.

His eldest son, born at Gordonstoun in 1648, was the prominent Quaker, writer and colonial governor Robert Barclay. A staunch defender of Quakerism, he was the author of a number of influential works including the 1673 *Catechism and Confession of Faith*.

This was at a time when Quakers were frequently subjected to persecution, including imprisonment, forcing many to flee British shores to seek new lives for themselves in what was then the British colony of America.

Imprisoned himself for a time, he nevertheless came to enjoy the favour of King James II and, through his influence and that of the leading Quaker William Penn – who would gave his name to the American state of Pennsylvania – Robert was appointed governor of New Jersey.

An absentee governor, however, he acted through a number of deputies, spending his remaining years at the family estate in Kincardineshire where he died in 1690.

Married to fellow Quaker Christian Mollison,

a daughter of Gilbert Mollison of Aberdeen, he had three sons and four daughters.

His second eldest son David, born in 1682 and later known as David Barclay of Cheapside, was the Quaker, businessman and banker who became a leading linen merchant in London.

He died in 1769, while his banking interest came through his second marriage to Priscilla Freame, daughter of the banker John Freame.

The father of fourteen children through his first marriage to Anne Taylor and Priscilla Freame, his second eldest son was David Barclay, born in 1729 and better known to posterity as the Quaker, banker and philanthropist David Barclay of Youngsbury.

Inheriting shares through his step-mother in the Freame Bank which her father co-founded, he and his brother John laid the foundations for what became Barclays Bank, now known as the multi-national investment bank and financial services company Barclays plc.

With business interests in a Jamaican estate, true to his Quaker beliefs he famously freed the slaves who toiled there and also arranged better futures for them in Pennsylvania. Not quite in keeping with Quaker teetotal beliefs, he also acquired a large brewing interest in England through H. Thrale and Company, later Barclay Perkins and Company and which merged with Courage Brewery in 1955.

Purchasing the manor of Youngsbury, Hertfordshire, in 1769 and having the noted landscape designer Capability Brown introduce a serpentine lake to the estate, he died in 1809.

In the contemporary world of business, Sir David Barclay, along with his brother Sir Frederick, was one of the Barclay billionaires more commonly known as the Barclay Twins or Barclay Brothers.

Born within ten minutes of each other in London in 1934 to Scottish parents, their father was a travelling salesman – while the only way in which to distinguish them was that Sir David, who was right-handed, parted his hair to the left, while his left-handed brother parts his to the right.

From modest roots, they progressed to accrue their fortune through a diverse range of business interests including property, retail and media.

Leaving school when aged sixteen, they worked for a time in the accounts department of the General Electric Company (GLC) before setting up as painters and decorators and then as tobacconists and confectioners on the edge of Kensington, London.

Notably reclusive in later life, the brothers first began to attract attention in 1955 when David Barclay married Zoe Newton, one of the most photographed models of her time and the 'face' of the Dairy Council advertisement 'drinka pinta milka day'.

Having vastly expanded their business interests, in 1983 they went further by purchasing the brewing and shipping group Ellerman for £45m, later selling the brewing division for £240m and using the proceeds to buy London's famous Ritz Hotel in Mayfair in 1995.

A raft of other retail and property purchases added to their portfolio, while also first branching out into media in 1992 by buying the former *The European* newspaper.

Further newspaper publishing enterprises include the *Scotsman*, bought in 1995 and sold to Johnston Press in 2005 and, in 2004, what is now Telegraph Media Group that includes the *Daily Telegraph*, *Sunday Telegraph* and *Spectator* magazine.

In 1993, the brothers bought the lease of the small Channel Island of Brecqhou, building a mock-Gothic castle that is rarely, if ever, penetrated by the prying eyes of the media.

With their wealth estimated at £7billion in the *Sunday Times* Rich List 2020, part of the veil of secrecy surrounding their lives was lifted when a case began at the High Court in London that year.

The civil action was brought by Sir Frederick Barclay, who said he and his daughter Amanda were secretly 'bugged', over a period of time when they met in the conservatory of the Ritz Hotel by his brother David's sons Alistair, Aidan and Howard and Aidan's son Andrew.

The bugging is claimed to have been in connection with controversial plans for the sale of the Ritz, first opened by the Swiss hotelier César Ritz in 1906. The Grade II listed 5-star hotel was sold in March of 2020 to an unnamed Qatari investor for £750m.

The defendants admitted making secret recordings, but denied any conspiracy to damage any financial interest of Sir Frederick and his daughter, claiming their actions had been necessary to protect business interests from potential harm. They agreed to pay damages.

At the time of Sir David's death in January of 2021, the case had been under consideration with respect to possible breaches of data protection laws.

Chapter four:

On the world stage

Behind the camera lens, Paris Barclay is the American director, producer and writer responsible for a string of award-winning television series and shows.

Born in 1956 in Chicago Heights, Illinois, he worked as a copywriter and creative supervisor for a number of advertising companies before turning his talents towards television.

His credits as a director include *The West Wing*, *Blue*, *Smash*, *Cold Case*, *City of Angels*, *Law and Order*, *NCIS: Los Angeles* and *NYPD Blue* – winning Emmy Awards for Outstanding Director for a Drama Series for the latter.

President of the Directors Guild of America (DGA) from 2013 to 2017, he is also the recipient of three separate NAACP (National Association for the Advancement of Colored Persons Awards) for his work on *City of Angels*, *Cold Case* and *Smash*.

Not only an actor but also a talented artist and caricaturist, **Don Barclay** was born in 1892 in Portland, Oregon.

First appearing on the big screen in 1915 in *Keystone Cops* silent slapsticks and, nearly fifty years later, as Mr Binnacle in the Walt Disney *Mary Poppins*, early in his career he worked a two-man comedy routine with his English-born flatmate Archie Leach – later to gain fame as the actor Gary Cooper.

While on film sets, Barclay would while away time between takes by executing caricatures of fellow actors.

So accomplished were these that, earning more by selling them than as an actor, he became a full-time artist – producing hundreds of caricatures of celebrities including Stan Laurel, Lou Costello, Bob Hope, Jimmy Durante, Frank Sinatra and Joan Crawford.

Many of these featured on ranges of ceramic souvenir mugs which, along with some of his rare original paintings, have been much in demand at auction since his death in 1975.

Born in 1916 in Williton, Somerset, Mary Biddulph was the English actress of theatre, television and film better known by her married name **Mary Barclay**.

Graduating with a double first in Classics

from Cambridge University she was nevertheless turned down for a position in the Civil Service.

Working in London in an Oxford Street music store, she lodged for a time with Clara Davies, mother of the Welsh composer and actor Ivor Novello – with one condition of her stay being that she regularly take out Clara's empty gin bottles.

But Clara also taught her to sing and play piano and, just before the outbreak of the Second World War in 1939 she enrolled in the Guildhall School of Music and Drama.

Marrying the future BBC film editor Richard Barclay about this time, she immigrated with him to Canada at the end of the war and, in 1948, made her television debut in *Sins of the Fathers*.

Also having appeared on stage on Broadway, she returned to Britain in 1956 and, in the 1960s, featured in the role of Stella Dane in the popular *Crossroads* television soap – with a number of big screen credits following in the 1970s, most notably *A Touch of Class*, opposite George Segal and Glenda Jackson.

With further television credits including *Spy Trap* and *Secret Army*, she died in 2008.

Born in Plymouth in 1984 but raised in New

Zealand and later settling in Australia, **Emily Barclay** is the actress whose role in the 2004 *In My Father's Den* won her the Most Promising Newcomer Award at the British Independent Film Awards.

The recipient of the AFI (Australian Film Institute) Award for Best Actress for the black comedy *Suburban Mayhem*, she is also an ambassador for Australia's animal protection group Voiceless.

A direct descendant of David Barclay of Youngsbury, referred to in the previous chapter, **Humphrey Barclay** is the British television comedy producer and executive born in 1941 in Dorking, Surrey.

Employed by BBC radio early in his career, he was responsible for putting together the team that, starting in 1964, produced the comedy show *I'm Sorry, I'll Read That Again*, while, in 1977, working for LWT (London Weekend Television), he won a BAFTA nomination for Best Situation Comedy for *Two's Company*.

Forming Humphrey Barclay Productions in 1983 and producing shows including the media satire *Hot Metal* and the black sitcom *Desmond's*, other positions he has held include development executive for Celador Productions.

Pulling the strings in the entertainment world, **David Barclay**, is the British Master Puppeteer born to an English father and Scottish mother.

Also a director and producer of animatronic and animation projects for film and television, his first major work was chief puppeteer for the character Yoda in the 1980 *Star Wars* film *The Empire Strikes Back*.

Recognised as being at the cutting edge of animatronic puppetry, he has collaborated with the American puppeteers and animator Jim Henson and Frank Oz in projects including the 1982 film *The Dark Crystal*.

In the highly competitive world of sport, **George Barclay**, born in 1876 in Milton, Pennsylvania, has a particular claim to fame.

Having played Major League Baseball for the Boston Beaneaters and St Louis Cardinals and renowned for his vanity over his looks and eye for the ladies, it is nevertheless in the sport of American football that he has left a legacy.

This is through his invention of the first-ever protective football helmet, designed by Barclay to prevent players sustaining unsightly cauliflower ears during the rough and tumble of the game.

Originally fashioned by a saddle-maker with strips of leather harness padding, it made its debut at a game in 1896, but helmets based on the design were not made mandatory by the National Football League (NFL) until 1941 – 32 years after his death, aged only 30.

In the equally rough and tumble of rugby union, **John Barclay** is the Scottish player who won 76 caps playing for his country between 2007 and 2019.

Born in Hong Kong in 1986 and educated at Dollar Academy, Clackmannanshire, where he captained the school's 1st XV, he has also played for Edinburgh Rugby.

In the world of music, Édouard Ruault was the French music producer of singers including Charles Aznavour, Dalida and Jacques Brel better known as **Eddie Barclay**.

Born in Paris in 1921 and the founder of Barclay Records, he collaborated with Aznavour as writer on songs including *Quand tu m'embrasses (When You Hold Me)*, while also launching the careers of other stars including Mireille Mathieu and Eddie Mitchell.

He died in 2005 while, referred to by the media as "Bluebeard" because of his many marriages, nine in total, the officiating registrar at one wedding famously remarked: "Ah good day, Monsieur Barclay, what a pleasure to see you yet again."

Born in the Calton district of the east end of Glasgow in 1932, **James Barclay** was the Scottish journalist, novelist and playwright whose plays continue to attract audiences to the city's Pavilion Theatre since first staged in the 1970s.

It was while working as a reporter for the *Daily Record* newspaper that he entered a competition run by the theatre to write a play.

His winning entry was *The Bigot*, set in his native city and infused with what became his trademark of wryly observed humour.

Turning to full-time writing, his book *Paras Over The Barras*, published by Lang Syne Publishing, was adapted for stage after Barclay was encouraged to do so by Pavilion Theatre manager Iain Gordon.

So popular were his plays that at one time the theatre had three – *The Bigot*, *Paras Over The Barras* and *Aggie's Anniversary* – running over three consecutive months.

The recipient in 2008 of the Lord Provost's Literature Award at a ceremony in Glasgow City Chambers, he died in 2019.

In the world of contemporary art, **Claire Barclay**, born in Paisley in 1968, is the Scottish artist of mediums including sculpture, printmaking and installation whose work was the subject of a solo exhibition at the Tate Modern, London in 2004 and at Tramway Gallery, Glasgow in 2017.

Recognised as a pioneering comic-book artist, **Violet A. Barclay** was the American illustrator born in Manhattan in 1922. Also known professionally as Valerie and also by her married name Valerie Smith – she adopted 'Valerie' as the spelling of her forename after the actress Valerie Hobson.

Attending Manhattan's School of Industrial Art and the School of Visual Arts, her first full-time job in the profession was as a staff 'inker' for *Timely Comics*, the forerunner of *Marvel Comics*, working under legends in the field including Stan Lee as her editor and artist Dave Gantz.

With work including, from 1942 to 1948, *Super Rabbit*, much of her input went uncredited.

But due recognition came after 1949 when she embarked on a highly productive freelance career. working for a number of publishers including D.S. Publishing and American Comics Group and mainly in the romance genre.

She died in 2010, while in 2017 she was the posthumous recipient of the Inkwell Awards Special Recognition Award.

In the esoteric realms of astrology, **Olivia Barclay** was the British practitioner of the ancient art recognised as having been largely responsible for a major revival of its traditional forms.

Born in Essex in 1919, it was not until 1990, when aged 71 and after many years of study and tuition of others, that she published the best-selling *Horary Astrology Rediscovered* – with 'horary' the name of a technique believed to have been practised back through the dim mists of time by the Babylonians, Egyptians, Persians and Greeks.

The founder of the Qualified Horary Practitioner (QHP) correspondence course, with students from all over the world and the recipient in 1991 of the Professional Astrologers Incorporated Award for 'outstanding contribution to astrology' and recognised as having transformed it from obscure occultism to mainstream practice, she died in 2001.